How to "Primp" Life

*"The Prim and Proper Guide
For Young Girls and Young Ladies"*

"Here is the young girls and young ladies guide to becoming prim and proper."

Jasmine S. Jones &
Keeyma D. Beckley

UWriteit Publishing Company
Goldsboro, NC USA
www.uwriteitpublishingcompany.com
www.waituntilmarried.org

How to "Primp" Life by Jasmine S'. Jones & Keeyma D. Beckley / W.A.I.T.
Copyright © 2012 by Jasmine S'. Jones & Keeyma D. Beckley / W.A.I.T.

ALL RIGHTS RESERVED

ISBN: **ISBN-13: 978-0615656434 (UWriteIt Publishing Company)**
ISBN-10: 0615656439

First Printing June – 2012

NO PART OF THIS BOOK MAY BE REPRODUCED IN ANY FORM, BY PHOTOCOPYING OR BY ANY ELECTRONIC OR MECHANICAL MEANS, INCLUDING INFORMATION STORAGE OR RETRIEVAL SYSTEMS, WITHOUT PERMISSION IN WRITING FROM THE COPYRIGHT OWNER/AUTHOR

Unless otherwise indicated, Scripture quotations in this book are from the King James Version of the Bible.

This publication is designed to provide information in regard to the subject matter covered. It is published with the understanding that the authors are not engaged in rendering legal counsel or other professional services. If legal advice or other professional advice is required, the services of a professional person should be sought.

Printed in the U.S.A.

We dedicate this book:

To girls all over the world that is in search of something bigger than themselves. This book is also dedicated to our organization W.A.I.T. (We Are Inactive Teens), founded by Ministers Dexter and Petula Jones and launched by Jasmine Jones. Here to promote the cause of abstinence and celibacy to prevent teen pregnancy to better our youth.

Foreword By:
Keeyma D. Beckley and Jasmine S. Jones

My name is Lekeeyma Denise Beckley and I am one of the authors of this profound book. I am a senior at Wayne School of Engineering. When I first started writing this book it started out as something to do when I was bored and I never thought that it would be used and turned into a legit book. Advice is something me and Jasmine have always been good at giving and now we have the chance to do it worldwide.

Hi, my name is Jasmine Jones and I am the co-author of this profound book (like my sister mentioned above). I am a senior at Wayne Early Middle College High School. My sister had begun writing these rules on life which was basically our girl sessions on paper; I knew it was gold so we had to make it visible for the world to see. I believe that girls have the power to make the world a better place and this book will help them to do so. We as girls sometimes get sidetracked by obstacles in life such as boys, school, drama, etc.

My sister and I are here to help and guide our fellow young ladies to a better life, just as we are continuously learning ourselves. Read our prim and proper guide so your life can be primped too.

Introduction

Upon reading this book, I know you were thinking... what does "Primp" mean? If you weren't thinking that... we are going to tell you anyway. The definition of primp is to dress or groom with elaborate care. Hence, when we say "how to 'primp' life" then we mean the process of making life as beautiful as it can be. Since we are young ladies we are already good at making stuff pretty. Therefore, adding this book to your collection, shelf, book-bag, or even your purse will primp you into the ultimate prim and proper young lady. As a young lady it is important that you carry yourself as such, this includes your grades, social life, your manners, and how you treat others. Now, not that my sister and I are perfect (because we are definitely NOT) but, we wrote this book to help others learn from our experiences and even save some heartache, pain, and embarrassment.

Since we are still growing teenagers we have included advice from others into the book as well. Grab some pizza, water (because soda isn't healthy), and some friends and read this girl talk guide. It may even remind you of some of your own conversations. Enjoy!

Preface

Brief words of advice from teens just like us

- "Don't let life get the upper hand on you." **Shaykera Jones**

- "You can do anything if you try once. If you try something and you failed, at least you tried." **Cashmir Fountain**

- "Before you can love someone else, you must first love yourself!" This can get you through all your struggles: via **Keeyma D. Beckley and Jasmine S. Jones, Shaqorie Jones**

- "Continue to be true to yourselves. Don't do things for attention do things to better your life?" **Keema Jones**

- "To come to terms with life you must accept it first. Analyze it, and then remember to learn from it." **Keema Jones**

- "When heart break comes your way don't let it phase you because one heart break is

God's way of saying he has something better coming your way." **Akilah Carter**

- As the age old saying goes, "Don't let your good rest, until your good becomes better, and your better becomes best."
Jasmine S. Jones

- "No matter how sad your life or your story is, there is always someone else's life or story that is worse so appreciate the sunny days and build up the sad ones." **Jasmine S. Jones**

- "When you're young fashion isn't just clothing, it is a way of life, an expression of love, and a bit of rebellion."**Jasmine S. Jones**

- "Being loved does not mean that you're perfect." **Keeyma D. Beckley**

Primping Life & Its Consequences

1. **Primp Rule Number 1:** You must <u>NEVER</u> break the Primp rules for any male or anybody (Unless of course you're of **dating age** and know they are the one, in that case…GO FOR IT)!
    a. **Breaking this rule could result in the following**: Feeling dumb (because he wasn't about nothing) or because that particular person wasn't a true friend (because now you're feeling dumb).

2. **Primp Rule Number 2:** Always keep this quote in mind and abide by it, live by it, and breath it! I _____ (insert name) don't stress them, I just next them, and pretend I never met them.
    a. I know this seems harsh but this rule is vital to not only males but even other people in your life. **Breaking this rule could result in the following:** Tears (and I'm not talking tears of joy), heartbreak (smh), giving him a second chance (trust me the sequels always suck), stress and of course doubt (which

may come with panic).

3. **Primp Rule Number 3 :** Never contact a guy first rather it be via social sites , text , phone, email , video chat or letter (but I mean who still writes those) unless he request it. No matter how cute he is, fight the urge, eat a snack–CAUTION: do not overeat!!), turn your phone off and give it to your mom (because you will not get it back from your mom anytime soon) and do something to preoccupy your time. Make him think that you have a life that doesn't revolve around him.
    a. **Breaking this rule could result in the following:** Feeling dumb or sad (if he doesn't contact you back), anger (at yourself and him for being stupid), sprung or butterflies (when he does contact back), upset (when he stops talking to you randomly…this may also come with regret…which is never a good thing).

4. **Primp Rule Number 4:** Don't get to attach to a male! If you haven't notice they leave quickly.
    a. **Breaking this rule could result in the following:** Heartbreak (when he leaves), Tears and or what-ifs (example: If I would have done this would he have stayed), regret, the Detachment process (when you want to move on and you're trying but you want to talk to him at the same time, never a good feeling.)

5. **Primp Rule Number 5:** This one is more of a life rule...It's very important to always remember this one too. Like seriously if you don't remember nothing else you read, remember this...Are you ready for the WORLD'S GREATEST advice ever known to man...okay *deep breath * **Forget people's opinion of you !** I try not to use profanity it's not very lady-like or at least that's what my Grand mother would say.

a. **Breaking this rule could result in the following:** Changing for others (umm…aka FAKE!!) feeling bad and actually caring about what others think **(that is NEVER good).**

6. **Primp Rule Number 6:** Another life rule that can apply to the male species or to people in general. Do whatever makes you happy, you have one life use it wisely! Some young people would say Y.O.L.O and some older people might say Carpe Diem or Seize the Day! Life is short, might as well live it up…Right?? **(in a smart way)**
    a. **Breaking this rule could result in the following:** Being miserable, being a people pleaser, Changing and conforming to what others **THINK** you should be…I hope you notice I put an emphasis on think.

7. **Primp Rule Number 7:** <u>Nerds and good girls shall inherit it all.</u> I don't know about you all but that nice guy finish last

(in this case nice girl) it maybe be true and we might finish last but in the end we will finish with it all...Remember that and keep the faith.

8. **Primp Rule Number 8**: Whatever a guy can do a girl can do too, but here's the catch...we can do it...in heels ;) Don't take no for an answer especially because you're a young lady. Push for it, fight for it and win it all with style and grace just like a lady should.
    a. **Breaking this rule could result in the following:** Lost opportunities, regret, what-if, depression, extra pounds as a result of depression and ice-cream eating and of course breaking your neck if you took my heels joke literally and try to play football in heels, if so I'm not liable and if you didn't get hurt...you are a Boss Lady for sure.

9. **Primp Rule Number 9**: Save yourself for the right one!! (Which in anyone's case

should come in marriage... but it doesn't happen in all cases?)

    a. **Breaking this rule could result in the following things:** Unwanted Pregnancy, STD's, feeling stupid because ole boy didn't care about you and your life in the 1st place, attachment (unnecessary), feeling lousy, depression, tears, what-if's, regrets, and feeling lost and confused, and also defying the one thing that no one can take from you that makes a woman as special as we are).

10. **Primp Rule Number 10:** Do not live your love life based on fairy tales!! (TV be having you trippin' though) If you haven't noticed fairy tales aren't real. Also, there are good guys out there but no one is a perfect prince who either comes to sweep you off your feet to take you to their castles or is there a rat turned into a prince once he's kissed .... Therefore we should set our standards

realistically. So dream for your dream guy just don't expect the perfect story with it.

    a. **Breaking this rule could result in the following:** Being forever alone, being attached to your story instead of a real person, losing an actually potential good dude (there are some of them left... idk where they are so don't ask).

11. **Primp Rule Number 11:** Being single isn't really that bad, don't let these people fool you into thinking relationships are easy peasy lemon squeezy.... because they are not. This is why (HEED: THE FOLLOWING ADVICE IS VITAL TO YOUR LIFE, YOU NEED THIS!) Education is key! It is your meal ticket (even fast food ain't cheap no more because there frozen strawberry lemonade is $3! I got strawberries and lemons at the house!) You can't be about your business in college if you're broke, running after a man, and worrying about

him and his psychological issues (because of course he has some). In other words get your paper boo boo but get it the right way… be single enjoy your life go to college get your career and your 3 story house and your prince will come (but remember rule #10 not a literal prince)

   a. **Breaking this rule could result in the following:** loneliness, regret, unstable living, not accomplishing your dreams or postponing them, and wasted time (Oh gosh I hate wasting time!)

12. **Primp Rule Number 12:** Contrary to popular belief, complexion and race really has nothing to do with the guy. For example, white boys are better than black boys or red-bones are first choice. This is garbage! No matter what color they are personality is key. He can be as white as snow and still act like homeboy down the street, and to all you guys out there she can be the exact definition of a red-bone and still not be "wifey type" (cough

cough). In other words do not be pulled into the race hype factor, if you're with someone like what their personality brings and not their appearance.

    a. **Breaking this rule could result in the following:** disappointment, shock, feeling dumb, lost hope, and ultimately immaturity. (CAUTION: CHANGING RACES IS NOT THE ANSWER dudes take heed if you're reading this)

13. **Primp Rule Number 13:** Anything worth having is worth fighting for so if a dude really likes you… HE WILL WAIT!!! (For sex and a RELATIONSHIP). Caution dudes are impatient, and it doesn't even have to be with the major stuff… it can be with baby steps too such as relationships or going on a PROPER date (NO SNEAKING OUT THE HOUSE TO SEE A MOVIE YOU DON'T CARE ABOUT IN THE FIRST PLACE). Therefore a guy with your best interest at heart will wait an eternity just to be with his princess

(and as girls don't literally wait an eternity life is too short see rule #6). If he can't wait for a simple date then he won't wait for things that really matter, demand respect you're a lady you deserve it. (For further advice talk to a mother figure they know this stuff).

    a. **Breaking this rule could result in the following things happening:** 2-week relationships, unnecessary social site drama, wasted time, and of course feeling dumb (as stated in all our other rules, hope you read them).

14. **Primp Rule Number 14:** Style is everything. #SWAGG! I'm not saying break your bank account for clothes you don't have money to pay for, but I'm saying express who you are through style so people know who you are! If you rock snapbacks and skinnies DO IT! If you rock rainbow colors and jewelry DO IT! If you rock shades and 3-inch heels DO YOU BOO BOO!

a. **Breaking this rule could result in the following:** Not being you (also called FAKENESS), not being happy (also called DEPRESSION), and not being the creative young lady God intended (also called BLASPHEMY).

15. **Primp Rule Number 15:** You will never have the perfect body (yea I said go ahead and admit it), but you can have your perfect body (that don't give you all an excuse to go gaining unnecessary weight and getting diabetes and things so put down that milky way and go get an apple because it is all about being healthy). Don't always find something wrong because someone else thinks it's not right. Be you and who God created you to be. So if you're a size 1 but eat 10 pounds worth of food everyday then do you! If you're a size 10 be thick and beautiful. Just be healthy and hold your head high , put on some heels (or in my case converses) and be happy)

    a. **Breaking this rule could result in the following:** low self-esteem (You don't want that!! Trust), over training when working out, eating disorders, or just unnecessary doubt for yourself, and it can also cause you to be a party pooper.

16. **Primp Rule Number 16:** When you're down and out go online and watch you some comedy from some of your favorite comedians or whatever floats your boat… and just LAUGH. Momma always said the more you laugh the healthier you are and guess what … THEY ARE RIGHT! No need in having a pity party, laugh to yourself and relax.
    a. **Breaking this rule could result in the following:** depression, self-absorbing attitude, and missing out on some funny mess lol.

17. **Primp Rule Number 17:** You are a lady act as such (for all you ratchet females out there… no offense).

a. **Breaking this rule could result in the following:** Looking ghetto, being loud as all for no reason, being too "real" (for all you people who don't believe in the appropriate term honest), and being talked about by females you trust and don't trust (Key: everyone isn't your friend... which brings us to our next rule)

18. **Primp Rule Number 18:** KEEP A SMALL CIRCLE! The definition of small circle is not 8 of your friends who crash parties together. A small circle would be defined as you and your bestie aka the one who is like your sister, the female that actually cares about you and your future and vice versa. In some exceptions a small circle can be three friends, but because everyone keeps secrets this only works with guys. Therefore only keep who you need by your side because everyone that you may need...may not need you.

a. **Breaking this rule could result in the following:** Future Trust Issues, High School drama, fights with your "main chicks" (Key: they really wasn't your friend to begin with), and the wrong path for yourself.

19. **Primp Rule Number 19:** Independence is Key! Why is it key you may ask? …. Well you have to let people know (especially over egotistic males) that you don't need them. This doesn't mean become hard and closed minded and closed hearted. This means assert yourself, be self-sufficient and not passive, and go for what you want. P.S. You and God are the only ones that make your dream come true (if you didn't know that already).
    a. **Breaking this rule could result in the following:** Dependency on the wrong people (such as an abusive boyfriend), getting taken advantage of, getting your feelings hurt, being

misunderstood (that is a horrible feeling! Trust me).

20. **Primp Rule Number 20:** Always have confidence and in the event that you don't have confidence FAKE IT!! How do you fake it you ask? You put on a smile and go about your business, whatever your business may be. Being polite in the face of adversity is as vital to your life as keeping that lip gloss on deck (you know ashy lips ain't cute). Don't be arrogant but be confident, carry yourself with grace and beauty and keep that beautiful smile like a young lady should.

21. **Primp Rule Number 21:** Internet photos… Momma always said whatever you put on the internet will always be up there sooooo… Thou shalt not look ratchet because Karma will come back. If you're a lady you should act as such at all times. So let's put away the duck faces, the sitting on the sink, the deuces (that should have been put up), the purse

holding pose, the half-naked sports bra looks (yes, sports bra are still revealing), the butt-outs at your girl's sleep over, the push up pose (That's when your boobs are all exposed and made to look bigger than they really are), etc.

   a. **Breaking this rule could result in the following:** Embarrassment, being talked about in a negative way, and the wrong and overly sexual approach from guys, not presenting yourself as a lady, and badly affecting your future (You want your past to make you not break you).

22. **Primp Rule Number 22:** NO Twerking for Likes! In other words, twerking is degrading for many reasons and is not appropriate to repeatedly post on the internet. In case you didn't know twerking originated in the strip club so, young women shouldn't objectify themselves to that standard. It's okay if

you're just with your friends playing around but rise above it in proper settings to be a proper young lady. As my sister always says, there's a time and a place for everything.

    a. **Breaking This Rule could result in the following:** Dudes over-sexualizing you, bad reputation for your future and your present, lost respect (no offense).

23. **Primp Rule Number 23:** The *B***** word is a *BAD* word. I know you been hearing this all your life but let's break it down to you. Guys nowadays will call you a *Bad B***** and people find this cute… but it's NOT -_- . For all the girls that think B**** means the following acronyms (**B**eautiful, **I**ntelligent, **T**alented, **C**aring, **H**onest, ~or~ **B**eing, **I**n, **T**otal, **C**ontrol, **H**oney), it doesn't mean that. It is a derogatory term and its definition is a female dog and no acronym, rapper, boyfriend, or photo edit is going to change that. Remember you are a lady.

24. **Primp Rule Number 24:** We know this is a touchy subject but.... whatever you have FAITH in; believe in it to the fullest. Whether its faith in your religion, your education, you, your parents, or your wildest dreams believe in it, live by it, and represent it.

    a. **SN:** For the Christians, as Christians ourselves we know it's hard to live by the word and represent at places like school, parties, etc. but as a young Christian it's even more difficult so our advice to you is to uphold the standard and be the best Christian you can be and that you know Jesus would intend you to be. Don't be fake but don't be a nonbeliever either.

25. **Primp Rule Number 25**: The internet does not need your life story; your business isn't for everyone to know. Of course we're referring to... Social sites.

People judge you based off what you do and what they see because no one really truly knows you and the internet is not how they get to know you. The best way to cut down on the rumors circulating about you is to keep your business off the internet. I know people use the internet as a way to vent but you can't really vent if everyone is taking your words out of context. Besides there are other ways such as find a hobby that makes you happy (e.g. writing, music, sports, school work, church, dancing, etc...). And another thing, do not deny yourself and your good intentions for Social site likes and retweets. No one really cares about your randomness and unnecessary post! For Example, LMS (like my status) if you single, LMS if you faithful, LMS if you cute if not I am going to call you out, Repost if you love your mom, Repost if your age is off the clock, LMS if you love God if not keep scrolling, LMS if you would die for your mom … if not she dies tonight. All of these are unnecessary and stupid! Trust me God doesn't care about statuses and he loves people on and off Social sites so please get it together (cuz yall ain't bout that life).

    a. **Breaking this rule could result in the following:** Fake friend (who wants that), people who act like they care but really don't, addiction to social networks, entertainment for other people (yeah we be laughing at you), looking very emotional and looking very unintelligent (a real lady always act intellectual)

26. **Primp Rule Number 26:** Popularity… this is not even remotely important to your life or your future. I know you're saying what that's not true but it really is. Popularity is something you have to work to get and to keep and in doing that you might lose touch of your real self. Why work so hard to keep friends that aren't even going to be in your future when you can work hard to obtain your

goals for your future? Because we all know that nerds is where it's at! You know that washed-up dude that still think he is a football player when he isn't; yeah he used to be popular.

    a. **Breaking this rule can result in the following:** Denial, regret, temporary friends (aka fake people), temporary happiness, mixed personalities, pipe dreams and pregnancy. (Refer to rule #7)

27. **Primp Rule Number 27:** Parents, the people who raised us, instilled so much in us, take us to practice, to the mall, pays our phone bills, cook and do all that good stuff and despite all that they do they still manage to get on our nerves …but here is where the rule comes in at. Nobody will ever love you like your parents, so TRY to Respect them no matter what. Nobody will ever have your back like them; NOBODY!! So no matter what happens and even if they say or act like they don't

care they still care more than anybody else.

   a. **Breaking this rule could result in the following:** Short days on Earth, being all alone , a part of you may seem missing (because you need your parents) and karma (your children might not respect you when you get older…you reap what you sow).

28. **Primp Rule Number 28:** Parents are also right no matter what. Yeah you know that boyfriend that you dated that you knew won't about nothing; yeah they were right about that. Or that friend that you knew was fake and your parents told you that and she backstabbed you, yeah they were right about that. Oh and that time you went to a restaurant and you wanted to **"try something new"** and they told you that you weren't going to like it and you didn't but you chocked it down anyway not to hear their comments, yeah they were right about that too. But

seriously parents are always right rather we want to admit it or not, so next time maybe you should hear them out, they might save you some trouble.

    b. **Breaking this rule could result in the following :** you looking stupid (yeah I said it) by doing your actions which are probably not well thought out (I mean we are pre-teen and teens)

29. **Primp Rule Number 29:** Moms, moms, moms... also known as mommy, ma, mother, me-ma, momma or whatever you call her they all describe the most important women in our lives (in some cases a mother figure). We love them, we hate them, we want to be like them, and we admire them. They are our back-bone, our support system, our nurse, our drill sergeant (that's for them early morning wake ups), our cook, our therapist, our chauffeur, our reality factor (they keep it real) and they are all that and so much more. No matter what we go through or

where life may take us our moms will always be by our sides, in our hearts and may even be in a bit of our personalities. They don't say you get it from your momma for nothing so respect them, love them and more importantly make them PROUD!!

30. **Primp Rule Number 30:** This is a tough one because this is something that we don't like to think about. So I guess we should start off by saying they aren't all bad because there are some stepparents that can truly make a positive difference **(shout out to my own)** but there are some who may not. So for those with the alcoholics, abusing, rumor starting, leeching step parents buy a IPod, pray about it and whatever you do don't disrespect your elders because though we may not want them there or understand why they are there people come into your life for a reason so learn your lesson and make the best of it.

a. **Breaking this rule could result in the following:** Prison, injury, broken hearts, broken homes and all the other drama on the countless lifetime movies.

31. **Primp Rule Number 31:** Our parents have lives too. So for all of you whose parents are divorced and are dating again try to remember that. Even though there may be a loss of attention and mixed emotions you have to remember you have your whole life ahead of you and your parents gave up some of their life for you, so let them be happy because they still love their honey bunches of oats (you).
    a. **Breaking this rule could result in the following:** Your parent not being happy and that is punishment enough. A happy parent makes a happy home.

32. **Primp Rule Number 32:** As females we need to learn how to control our emotions

sometimes. Please don't be like the women in the old movies who cry and faint over everything. We as women have come too far and have accomplished too much. You are a strong, independent young lady don't never forget it. Put away the envy, jealously, greed, doubt, anger, frustration laziness, the attitudes, the rolling of the eyes, the I don't care about him moments (even though you texting him right now), the omg moments that you knew was going to happen and the random cry moment for no reasons. Don't get me wrong crying is okay and emotions are natural but don't be a drama queen. Assert yourself, be strong and be a woman.

    a. **Breaking this rule could result in the following:** Being a drama queen, taking things to seriously, letting your emotions control your life and not being fun to be around.

33. **Primp Rule Number 33:** This is what makes you or breaks you, you know how they say your attitude makes or breaks you…yeah they were right. Irritation, impatience and stress are going to come with life but you must learn how to handle it. As a young lady you must handle the ups and downs of life with grace and coolness and do your best to remain lady-like. So put away the eye rolling (refer to rule 32 and the breaking of that rule applies to this rule also).

34. **Primp Rule Number 34:** Personality is a unique collection of attitudes, emotions, thoughts, habits, impulses and behaviors defining how a person typical behaves across a situation. (I know you like that psychology knowledge though) In other words your personality makes you…you so rep it to the fullest. For example, I am ridiculously organized or aka OCPD (Obsessive Compulsive Personality Disorder, basically means perfectionists and organized) but aye I rep to the fullest

and I embrace it for what it is and for who I am and I suggest you to do too. We aren't saying that you're perfect or that we are but embrace flaws for what they are and change them for the better. Furthermore, never let anybody affect how your feeling any day whether they fuss, fight, get an attitude, create drama, talk about you behind your back or to your face. You have to be the bigger person and keep your composure. God and you are the only ones that can control your day and your emotions, don't make it easy and let other people do it for you (I know it's hard but it's worth it after the day goes by).

    a. **Breaking this rule could result in the following:** Fakeness, incompleteness, feeling lost and missing out on opportunities (personality can you take you places)

35. **Primp Rule Number 35:** We probably know about as much as you do about

love since we too are young but that doesn't mean we can't give you a few pointers. Love is pure, it's God-given, it's understanding, it's patience and it's kind. If you love yourself others will love you too. Love conquers all, Love thy neighbor as thyself. Matthew 22:39 Love is positive and you want to be a positive person because good things come to positive people even though you may have to wait for it. That's pretty much all we can say about love because as we have stated before we are young too.

    a. **Breaking this rule could result in the following:** you getting no love (yep pretty much sums it all up).

36. **Primp Rule Number 36:** Self-esteem, yes this is a touchy subject but we must talk about it. Do you remember that day when that girl commented about your weight, hair, clothes, complexion and etc...? And everyone laughed at you, you felt alone but you played it off, but that night you

cried yourself to sleep. It's real and it happens to everybody rather you realize it or not and it's called low-esteem. We may not know how to conquer it because we go through it ourselves but it all goes back to love (rule #35), love who you are and embrace what you got. Find an outlet that helps you embrace who you are and go with it. For example, if you are being teased for your academic success and you may feel out casted use that as your motivation in school, make it far, go to college and make a difference like other famous people that succeeded.

    a. **Breaking this rule could result in the following:** Bitterness, loneliness, self-pity and exaggeration and much more damaging stuff but like I said we are learning to so just keep your head up.

37. **Primp Rule Number 37:** Saving yourself aka celibacy, abstinence or whatever you choose to refer it as is a difficult thing to

be in this time period and many don't understand so we are here to break it down. It's more than saving yourself, it's a commitment to God, yourself, a life saver, a spiritual emotion wall, and it is the doctor, and the house for the temple that is your body. It's a doctor because it protects your heart and body from all the bad things that may come from having sexual relations with someone who doesn't care about you or your well-being. It is a hard decision and you may not find a lot of people to support it but it is the best choice when it comes to saving your mind. It's not forever contrary to popular beliefs it's just until you find the right one with God's help. Your virginity is a gift that you and your husband should give to each other, it's special and you only have one. Sex is meant to be a beautiful, emotional occasion not a five minute Bing, bow and he never call again. Keep that in mind, a real man will wait for his lady.

a. **Breaking this rule could result in the following:** Unwanted Pregnancy, STD's, feeling stupid because ole boy didn't care about you and your life in the 1st place, attachment, pity, (unnecessary), depression, tears, what-if's, regrets, and feeling lost and confused, and also defying the one thing that no one can take from you that makes a woman as special as we are).

38. **Primp Rule Number 38:** College, the thing that we have been working our whole lives for, the magic word, the big key and for some the way out your parents' house. Whatever college is to you make it an academic experience as well as a life changing one. Don't party every night because that's not what it's designed for, go there with a plan in mind and achieve it. Remember this is your life, your money (aka your parent's money) and your education. In college

it's all about you, the teachers give you the work and you do it so stay on top of your game and do it big. Remember after college the real world starts and so does your life so make it a life worth living. P.S. we know school isn't for everyone just don't waste your life.

   a. **Breaking this rule could result in the following:** being a bum, not being a boss, misdirection to your future, a fall back plan, and lost opportunities.

39. **Primp Rule Number 39:** As ladies, we always forgive but never forget. This is actually a good thing, we realize that forgiveness is a difficult thing to have and to give but it's a process to have the strength to love those that hurt you. Remember forgiveness is like medicine it's hard to swallow but in the long run it helps. Try to forgive those who did you wrong and be the bigger person because at the end of the day you have to answer for yourself and nobody wants a heavy heart.

a. **Breaking this rule could result in the following:** regret, anger, bitterness, a heavy heart, grudges, and it will affect your genuine view of that person. (people do change you know even if it takes a while)

40. **Primp Rule Number 40:** Music vital for us young people. We have all had those days where we are having a bad day and we put our headphones in but we are sad slow music is the way to go. So put away all the love songs and put on some upbeat music, (in my opinion Gospel too because it might help you forget the hurt). Just remember music is supposed to be uplifting so sleeping with a broken heart and listening to the song at the same time might not be a good idea. Music is what you feel and how you feel… so feel beautiful.
    a. **Breaking this rule could result in the following:** Being somewhere in the dark crying; listening to a love song, eating ice cream, and

rambling about your life. Also, unnecessary tears, pain/heartache, random anger, and Hating a song just because it reminds you of a situation even though you know you love that song... no unnecessary hate for songs.

41. **Primp Rule Number 41:** So we have to use a rule to discuss how music can minimize our originality. I know you're wondering what we mean by this so here are some examples so think about what we are saying because I know we aren't the only people who have noticed. Example one have you noticed how nobody had a "Mr. Wrong or boo thang" till the song came out. No girl really started claiming she had a breaking point till famous singers made songs that say such things and nobody would openly claim trust issues till famous singers made it sound cool. Yes we all have done this at least once and I know music is meant to inspire us and help us express

our feeling and tune the world out but also remember being ORIGINAL is a part of expressing yourself.

a. **Breaking this rule could result in the following:** Being fake, unoriginal and not expressing your true self. Let music inspire you not change your whole way of thinking.

42. **Primp Rule Number 42:** The Bestie Moment aka the vital period of time where you and your sister, best friend, cousin, partner-in-crime, (whatever or whoever that person is), have the random-est, silliest, and best moments ever that make life memorable. The correct way to have these bestie moments are through shopping trips (of course), sleep-overs, and girls' night out. This is another way to relieve stress and get those necessary laughs in with young ladies that are very important to your life. What you can't say around parents, adults, or even others your age, you can always share with your best friend. They should understand, agree, argue,

disagree, laugh, and at the end of the day be there for you. Idk what I'd do without my twin sister aka best friend (who agreed to making this into a book by the way lol). Refer to rule #42 to know how this best friend is to act to make a proper bestie moment.

    a. **Breaking this rule could result in the following things happening:** Being misunderstood, having fake friends, feeling alone in this big ole world, and boredom (which is terrible and has been scientifically proven to kill because we all know when we get bored we do stupid stuff).

43. **Primp Rule Number 43:** Guy best friends. I know society has said that a guy and a girl can't be JUST friends this however is not true. A guy friend can be just that. A guy best friend can be just as important as a girl best friend. They can give you guy advice and help you understand the mind of a male which we

as females lack the true understanding of, they protect you , they love you, they call you pretty when you feel you look awful. They are just as important as your girl best friend I can't stress this enough(I myself I have a guy best friend), they do some of the same things that a girl best friend does and to have a girl best friend and a guy best friend by your side you might truly feel blessed.

    a. **Breaking this rule could result in the following:** Getting bad guy advice from your girl best friend because girls don't really understand guys. Plus guy best friends' rock.

44. **Primp Rule Number 44**: So I'm going to try to break this one down for you. So you have this guy best friend and you come to him with everything and one day some emotions start to fly and then BAM! You like your guy best friend and know you're panicking. Don't be alarm it happens to the best of us. Just remember

that it's normal to gain feelings for your guy best friend because they are so important to you and they are always there for you. Just because friends fall in love don't mean they are meant for you and that's also with any guy. So take your time with the decision to tell him, be sure of your feelings and follow your heart. And if he just wants to stay friends respect his decision.

   a. **Breaking this rule could result in the following:** Losing your best friend which is awful enough.

45. **Primp Rule Number 45:** So you may think having a big circle of people is what it's all about. For example in famous shows and even in some of the movies they have a group of three or more best friends and they tell each other their secret and everything is unicorns and rainbows but it's NOT!!! In reality when you have three or more best friends it's not that great. In the group the two main best friends who are going to make

everybody else feel left out regardless. They will always be that broken bond so you might as well just keep a close girl and guy best friend and call it a day. Trust me we know from personal experiences even if you do include the other person it won't be as glamorous as the movies makes it seems. So it's okay to get ready with just one best friend at least you know their real.

    a. **Breaking this rule could result in the following:** Secrets, rumors, unnecessary tension, hurt feelings, fake friends, two-faced people (smile in your face but talk about you when you leave) and just drama and a lot for no reason.

46. **Primp Rule Number 46:** You know that feeling you get when you are all happy and excited about a certain special someone and then all of a sudden those feelings go down the drain because he was leading you on? This is also called false hope (smh). False hope is when a

guy gets you all worked up because he can have your favorite qualities or just be like the best friend you've never had but turns out he is not about that life! In other words, he didn't even want close to a friendship. This is a sucky feeling! Our advice to you all to avoid this false hope is to keep your guard up and not get overwhelmed just because a guy may seem perfect, or he says and does all the right things because looks can be and will be deceiving. Be a strong little big girl and if things don't turn out as planned take it as a blessing disguised in a lesson (I had to do it and I got through it, so you will too). Girls can lead people on to, so please don't do this to anyone because whether a girl; or guy does this, it still brings the same pain. Say what you mean and mean what you say.

    a. **Breaking this rule could result in the following:** Denial, low self-esteem (due to you blaming yourself for his misleading ways), waste of time and energy, feeling stupid and feeling used, and being disappointed in general (which could possibly make you bitter toward males everywhere).

47. **Primp Rule Number 47:** **Trumpet Sounds** **the moment every girl dreams of having, the feeling that is indescribable, the moment that cannot be forgotten is none other than… BUTTERFLIES!**

The proper definition of butterflies can be described as a tingly feeling in your stomach, accompanied by a sense of relaxation through whole body, along with sweaty palms, a racing heart, and an instant feeling of nervousness but happiness. The butterflies we're describing come when you experience a kiss. Not just any kiss, this kiss would come from a person you care deeply about or someone who you likey likey!

You and this person would have some type of instant connection whether it is mental, spiritual, or physical. You would probably feel butterflies just from seeing this person or being around them. However it happens, or whenever it happens you can't plan it or even prepare for it. When you get butterflies they will just show up for that instant and you'll just know it was butterflies. This is very unexplainable so I hope you appreciate this explanation (lol). Don't rush the flutter though just let it come as life breezes and you find that special guy to share that special kiss and I'm pretty sure guys feels them too (I don't really know though, so don't ask lol).

   a. **Breaking this rule could result in the following:** You can't break this rule because butterflies are a firework of emotions, just don't feel like they are never going to come because they will. Just take your time and don't think on it.

48. **Primp Rule Number 48:** There are popular sayings that go… "Bros over Hoes", "We don't love em tho" (yes we know these sound illiterate but people say these things and believe them… mostly guys anyways). All these phrases

are disrespectful in a sense. Let's take "bros over hoes", whoever made this phrase... well we don't know what they had going on because what real guy would go with their friends over the females they like. Loyalty is important when dealing with friends, family, siblings, etc... but in this context it's stupid. They can use these phrases to justify wrong doings onto their girlfriends or to just avoid serious commitment. And the ever popular terms that degrade women or "we don't love em tho" (this is a Christian book) is basically putting material things over love and commitment. Overall, it's just media propaganda and real gentlemen do not uphold these sayings. It's almost like when girls say "Friends are forever and guys are whatever"... but a mature lady knows how to balance both and in vice versa so should a young man.

49. **Primp Rule Number 49:** Social sites names, all I can say is please stop the

madness. You may say oh I have a normal Social site name and we do too. But I have seen some names that had me like what the what. For example names like Tonya ImRisingAboveItAll Richardson is not attractive, your Social site name should not be your life story or a sentence. And please don't have a whole song lyric as you name, example MariahTheyCan'tTellMeNothingBecauseI BeezInTheTrap Jones or Keisha BabyImaBeYourMotivationSoDon'tStop Williams or a ghetto name like Shaquironisda2ChainzzIsMyFutureBaby DaddySoBoysDon'tHMUThompson.

These are not names of a lady and they aren't anything but entertainment for people on Social sites. It's okay to be creative but please try to be classy also. Now for other Social sites I shake my head at the ones I have seen, names such as @i_EatThecaptinCrunch (what a name) or @_SuckMyVans like seriously please get that together that is not classy at all and that's not a good name for a young lady. Please remember to hold yourself to high esteem at all-time even on the internet. (We are not liable for any of the names that we named in this rule; if this is your name I am sorry. We chose random to add some humor).

　　a. **Breaking this rule could result in the following:** Embarrassment, people laughing at you, being viewed as un-classy and seeming ignorant.

50. **Primp Rule Number 50:** We know you have heard this a million times before but because we are girls we must discuss this again. Hygiene is very important. Hygiene includes deodorant, brushing your teeth, clean nails, lotions, feminine odor, menstrual cycles, your hair and etc... Always stay fresh and keep different items in your purse and or school locker to help you remain fresh. Here is a mini-checklist that we have compiled for

personal hygiene: Mini-deodorant, lotion, lip-gloss, perfume, wet wipes, pad or tampons (just in case), mini-Kleenex, nail-file, mini-tooth brush and tooth paste, mints or gum, mini mouth-wash, floss, panty-lines, extra underwear and sweat to put in locker in case of emergency and even though this doesn't have anything to do with hygiene always try to carry $5 with you just in case you get hungry or have to take a cab home. If you don't want to carry these items in your purse having them in school lockers would be good too. Remember to always check yourself and make sure you smell like a lady should. (You know flowers, fruit, candy, fruit punch etc...)

    a. **Breaking this rule could result in the following:** Bad health, being teased, unpleasant odor, losing friends (fake ones because a real friend would tell you what's up), and embarrassment.

51. **Primp Rule Number 51:** As you may have heard a hairstyle personifies yourself. Momma always said one of the first thing's people look at when they see a lady is her hair. Even the bible says a woman's hair is her glory; *If a woman has long hair it is her glory to her for her hair is given to her for a covering 1 Corinthians 11:1.5* In that case we must always keep our hair in check so that we will make lasting impressions on those who do view us (Besides you may meet your future husband or future employer on the streets one day). When I say keep your hair in check, I mean keep your hair presentable to others but keep it true to your-self. If you have long hair and you pride yourself in that, don't cut it just because a bob cut is the latest style. If you have short hair don't feel less feminine because of that, rock it the best way you can. Whether it's short and trendy, long and luxurious, kinky and creative, wet and wavy, or you have exotic extensions your hair is you! Find the style that you

like and that looks good on you; because it's your head so treat it with respect. Keep your hair healthy whether that involves greasing it, moisturizing it, perming it, cutting it, clipping it, dying it, curling it, straightening it, flipping it, braiding it, shining it, pressing it, highlighting it, shampooing it frequently … you get the point! Do what needs to be done to keep yourself looking like the beautiful young lady you are. Now don't go fixing your hair like famous stars every time they make a new music video, be you and be beautiful (You better do it girl!).

    a. **Breaking this rule could result in the following:** Low self-esteem, untreated hair (looking like you don't care), missing opportunities, bad first impressions, missing out on natural beauty, missing out on glam and creativity (Life is short so if you want extensions then weave it up!), embarrassment.

52. **Primp Rule Number 52:** Aaaaaaaahh clothes, so important to a young girl's life

matter fact even a woman's life! Clothes is just as vital as music, it's a way to express yourself so the whole world can see you when not even the slightest person understand you. Fashion repeats itself but that doesn't mean you have to repeat everyone else's style. Clothes are there to mix and match, to colorize and coordinate, to rebel with and rejoice in. Like we said in rule #14, "Do you boo boo." In other words, pride yourself in the way you dress. Be comfortable but classy, be trendy but cute, be unique but not weird, being trendy may not be you so remember to be yourself, have confidence and strut it.

   a. **Breaking this rule could result in the following:** Lacking confidence, not expressing your-self, doing whatever seems popular and looking un-classy.

53. **Primp Rule Number 53:** Once again… here we go with the touchy subjects. This rule is especially for women of color. As

you all know in the African American culture there is a controversy between being lighter-skinned versus being dark-skinned or brown-skinned. As time goes by the media does nothing to stagnate this controversy. Therefore, as young ladies up in a technology based society we must know our own worth and embrace our own beauty and not get caught up in the hype of the media. What we're saying is you don't have to be a "red-bone" or "yellow-bone" to be pretty or worthy of acceptance. You don't have to be curvaceous with long hair to be accepted by the media. We're not downing anyone's skin color because as women of color we are all different shades and sizes and that alone makes us gorgeous in our own right. But shout out to the brown sugar's , the coffee-colored, the caramel skinned, the milk chocolate, the dark chocolate, the mocha's, the pecan/walnut colored, and bronze colored sister's. Don't allow your esteem to be reduced by media propaganda you are beautiful and so is the skin you are in. Being dark is not a burden and being light doesn't make your complexion a blessing. Use your looks to lift each other up and not tear each other down and a rapper's words aren't divine so don't take that too literal either.

   a. **Breaking this rule could result in the following:** Low self-esteem, doubt, second guessing yourself, continuing the stereotype, self-hate, and not respecting your heritage/culture.

54. **Primp Rule Number 54:** You know how when you're talking to a guy and all of a sudden he start calling you all these random cute nickname and it be having you tripping though thinking your special when he really say that to everybody. The commonly confused words are bae, boo, wifey, fb wifey, twifey, I wish you was my wifey, wifey type, babe, baby, RIDE or DIE, boo

thang/unofficial girl, lil mama, and sweetheart. By us being girls we have all been called one of these names by a guy but we must understand no matter how cute they sound to us they mean something deeper to and maybe less to them the majority of the time. Don't get offended at the words and don't get overwhelmed at the concept of it too. (the dictionary can explain the true definitions of the words better) Just try not to get upset or be confused if a guy calls you wifey and then the next day he goes with somebody else (dates them), take it as a lesson and remember one day a special guy will call you wifey and mean it till death do you part.

   a. **Breaking this rule could result in the following:** A broken heart, confusion, bragging with no real notion of the concept (for example, Oh he said I'm his boo for life and then two weeks later you don't even talk anymore) and false hope (refer to rule #45).

55. **Primp Rule Number 55:** Dealing with males is a trip. Sometimes it's hard to understand whether or not they are being honest especially when you question the things they do and the things you heard. So we have compiled a list of classic lies that we have heard some personally and some from friends: I don't know how she got my number I think my boys gave it to her, she just my sister, that's just my cousin, you the only one I messing, me and you forever bae, I never felt like this before, Forget the haters we going to ride for each other to the wheels fall off, nah I ain't hang up my phone died, nah I didn't know my ex was going to be there, I don't mess with her no more, your my everything, all I ever wanted (you ain't a rapper so stop it) and many, many more. And we aren't saying that every guys lies and that if a guy says this to you it's a lie. We are just giving a heads up and some advice, but follow your heart because as young women we the males we mess

with and we know when they are being honest or not. Just be careful.

56. **Primp Rule Number 56:** All relationships have their ups and downs and no relationship is perfect. However there are those relationships that are too up and down and we call this the on and off, the break up make up, or the rollercoaster. If you are in this type of relationship talk it out and make a decision on what yall want to do. Sometimes love or strong like isn't enough to sustain a relationship especially if the relationship is full of heart break and troubles. Remember you're too young and beautiful to be caught up with a bunch of drama and if you're the problem then maybe you should let him go because sometime love also means having the strength to give a person up. So the best advice on this that we can give is follow you heart and remember that you are still young and part of being a lady is knowing how to make good decisions.

a. **Breaking this rule could result in the following**: Mixed emotions, wasted time, unresolved problems, stress, relationship haters (those that say "ummm... why are you still with him"?) and confusion.

57. **Primp Rule Number 57:** Role models!! We all have them. The people that inspire us, somebody that we look up to. Rather it is your mom, a famous actor or actress, a political figure, singer etc...or whomever you choose to admire. But lately I have noticed how some young girls chose to admire a lot of reality TV show women and I'm not saying that they are all bad but reality TV isn't real. A true role model should be someone who is making a mark on the world, who is strong, kind, intelligent and beautiful in soul and mind. Throughout history women have overcame a lot in the way of women's rights and we are still doing such. So essential admire those who does good on and off the screen.

a. **Breaking this rule could result in the following:** Acting ghetto and un-classy for no reason, fighting for no reason and being something you're not.

58. **Primp Rule Number 58**: First things first, erase from your mind all the stereotypical images that come to mind when you think of the word… NERD. I know you are asking yourselves, why are they giving advice on being a nerd? Well we are doing so because if you haven't heard, as in rule #7, <u>**"The Nerd shall inherit the earth."**</u> What we mean is one who keeps their nose in the books and their mind in their school work and their heart with God shall attain all their dreams to better the world around them. A nerd does not have to be a lame, an outcast, or your typical television nerd. A nerd does not have to wear the ugliest clothes, or have the weirdest hairstyles, or be the one with the least amount of friends. This is the picture society paints

for us so we believe it. Don't fall into societies web of lies, being a nerd is not bad nor is it worse than being "the most popular girl in school." We aren't going to lie and say that being a "nerd" doesn't come with consequences like being teased, ridiculed, humiliated, hated on (Believe it or not people are actually jealous of good grades and the prospects of a bright future), and etc... We are just saying that there is absolutely nothing wrong with being an intellectual. Hence, the proper definition of a nerd is one who takes pride in their school work and is dedicated to a beneficial future. A nerd can be beautiful, classy, intelligent, intellectual, sociable, relatable, and a genius. We as nerds ourselves can honestly say a remarkable transcript is much more promising than a remarkable party night. Trust me we know from experience it may be hard to put aside common social deviances to promote your education but it's for the best. If you're anything like us there is nothing better than the feeling you get from accomplishing something yourself like getting an A in Calculus or whatever class you feel is difficult. Next time someone wants to down being a nerd you tell them what it really means!

Neat
Educated
Radiant
Devoted Diva

59. **Primp Rule Number 59:** Now this is something we dread, this is something we all want to avoid, this is something that can kill your grades and your time, and if you are in grades 9-12 than you know exactly what we are talking about. This is called *Trumpet Sounds*... **Procrastination**. According to any dictionary procrastination goes a little like this: "Putting off or delaying or deferring an action to a later time." This may seem harmless enough but trust us this act is detrimental! In other words, it

will and can kill you and your time especially when you have a 3-5 page research paper due tomorrow and you decide to do it the night before even though you had an entire two weeks to finish this oh so important paper! I know you are thinking to yourself... who is going to waste all that time to write a paper? Well, when you get to high school or college you will understand. Procrastination can deal with anything from waiting too late to get that new shirt you wanted, to putting off a big project, to even delaying doing a math worksheet to the point where you forget to do it. Matter of fact, we procrastinated on this book (only a little bit though) lol! All we're saying is learn from your mistakes and ours... do not procrastinate! My sister can tell you better than anybody if you're going to get something done do it now, and if you plan to do something later do it then! Trust us, that whole... "I have a whole week I'll do it later" always means never.

a. **Breaking this rule could result in the following:** Failed goals, no accomplishments, lack of discipline, crammed schedules, stress, regrets, wasted time, dissatisfaction with yourself, and ultimately never getting anything done! **WARNING: DO NOT PROCRASTINATE! DO IT NOW NOT LATER!**

60. **Primp Rule Number 60:** We always talk about what we want and expect in a boyfriend but we never seem to talk about what a guy might want in a girlfriend. So here goes the definition of a real girlfriend or at least some qualities that a real girlfriend should have. First off you should know when to fight your battles. Sometimes it's okay to fight and argue but sometime you must remember he is a male he wants to have control and the up hand so maybe sometimes you might have to fall back but that doesn't mean be a pushover. Remember to be kind, smart and listen to his little rants

about sports because it might not be important to you but to him it is, so make sure he feels important also. Also be sure to be understanding, classy, loyal and his shoulder to lean on if necessary. A relationship is meant to help you grow social, mental and spiritual no matter what gender you are.

   a. **Breaking this rule could result in the following:** A short relationship which also equals wasted time.

61. **Primp Rule Number 61:** We couldn't talk about what a real girlfriend should be like and leave out what a real boyfriend should be like. A real boyfriend should be kind, understanding, smart, sweet, caring and of course a good listener. But most importantly he should be a gentleman. You are a young lady who deserves the best. You deserve to be cherished and admired. You deserve to have your dinner paid for, to have the door opened, for a guy to hold your bags when you go shopping. To be honest you deserve that and so much more and I know you may think that will never happen, but it will, so just set your

standards high and follow your heart. A good guy will come along and sweep you off your feet. Remember if you act like a queen you will attract a king.

    a. **Breaking this rule could result in the following**: Low standards, unhappiness in relationships and missing out on the good guy that God has planned for you.

And *Trumpet Sounds* this brings us to the topic you've all been waiting for …BOYS. I know we have spoken on this throughout the book so far but now we're going deep into detail. This is a whole section dedicated to the different types of guys that you may have experience and for the youngins out there the guys you may encounter. So grab your highlighters, your best friends, a snack (preferably popcorn or candy), and open your eyes for reading and your mouth for laughing (because you will laugh). Sooo… *Drum Roll Please*!!

Introducing… Experienced by girls, written by girls, and shared to you by real girls (That's us the authors of the book … but anyway continue reading)

The Misters And Their Mishaps

Mr. Perfect aka Prince Charming

As females this is what we should all be aiming for, this is what movies teaches us, this is the perfect boyfriend of our dreams, the husbands your fathers want you to have, the man you're supposed to pray for, and the son-in-law mothers dream of... also known as your dream guy (this is where you say aaaaaaaw!) Just because this is the world's greatest man does not mean he exist. Not to be blunt but no one is perfect, so there's a reason you've only seen Prince Charming in movies. But the object of this particular guy type is to know that you don't have to settle for less but not to set unrealistic standards. Hence, if your dream is a super nice, super wealthy, and super attractive athlete who has a sensitive side... that's a bit farfetched. A more respectable dream would be a hardworking, established, and respectful guy who is the apple of your eye. Keep a look out for your prince charming but do not become obsessed with the idea of him, like we said in rule #10: These movies can have you trippin' though.

Mr. Player

This is the type us females should avoid and we don't know about you but WE ARE SICK OF IT!

WARNING: Mr. Player can seem like Prince Charming... at first, but later you will come to the shocking (and sometimes not so shocking) realization that your so called Prince Charming has about five other princesses.

You may have thought you were the only Princess in his life (due to classic lies referred to in rule #55) until you found out he had a whole list of other girls on deck. Mr. Player is very convincing and so smooth you may actually believe he is the one. If you do believe this don't be hard on yourself that's just how it goes, that is one of the reasons why the common Mr. Player has many Misses. Just don't be quickly persuaded by smooth talking, convincing explanations, good looks, cleverness, charm, and popularity. Those are the common traits of a player and the best thing to do is give it time to see if it's real and of course not to give up anything valuable like whole-hearted emotions, money, memories, and of course your virginity. We know the things a player may say is intriguing but remember it's probably recycled (as in not originally for your benefit alone). We don't know why some guys are players but all we can say is take heed. We can't promise you want run into one… we all do: we did, your mother did, and probably even your grandmother. Also, ladies are capable of being a player as well, so don't fall into that tricky trap either. Be smart, be alert, and be a lady.

Mr. Thug

Here we go with this one... he is just tragic! By tragic we mean, we do not know what exactly Mr. Thug is doing with his life. Unlike Mr. Player, he may not have charm or athletic support. Unlike Mr. Perfect, he may not be and all-around good guy. Most often Mr. Thug is laid-back, un-sober, and on an extreme end violent. This is the dude who probably isn't on your school sports team, definitely not in your honor society; In fact, he probably isn't at school most of the time. These types just don't have much going on in their life besides the typical things such as drugs, illegitimate money, bad influence of friends, and even illegitimate children.

Why are they such a threat then you may ask? Well... they often get girls due to their laid-back nature and reassuring confidence. Girls go for this type because they assert their independence and they have that "I do what I want, when I want attitude". For instance, Mr. Thug often carries respect from others and money (the wrong type of respect and money) and with a lady on his arm, she reaps those things too. Sort of like a bootleg celebrity life, in fact a rapper may come to mind because they often are this type. Think about it, a rapper has respect from his fans, "street credit", and money… but in some cases that's all they have and nothing else substantial like intellectuality, society approved respect, and morals (as in not stealing, not killing, no gang life, no unprotected sex). Which brings us back to the point at hand, Mr. Thug does not have anything important going on in his life therefore you should want better for yourself. WARNING: Mr. Thug often preys on the shy type because a shy lady normally isn't self-assertive or reassuring and since Mr. Thug prides himself in that… opposites tend to attract. If you are the shy type I suggest you avoid thugs at all costs… actually every girl should avoid thugs at all costs! I guess what we're saying is don't be tempted by the over-confidence and fooled by his cool demeanor; trust me they aren't about anything productive. In other words, they ain't bout' that life (that educational life).

Mr. Wannabe Thug aka Mr. Anksta

These are the types that TRY their hardest to be gangsta for whatever reason. As you heard us describe a thug in the above paragraph, a wannabe thug tries to mimic that. So… they may have a cool demeanor but it's all in vain because they are trying to be something they are not. Who wants a follower anyway? Leadership is a very important quality to look for in a guy, and a wannabe thug is far from a leader. They can be easily spotted as the guys who try to smooth talk you on Social sites, or maybe even in person. Even though we qualify "Mr. Anksta" in this category they are typically associates of thugs that follow the example of their friends which causes them to have a thuggish mentality even though they obviously don't want any real part of it. You know… the guys in school that put up a front and always "act" tough? Try to avoid these types at all costs because no one wants a faker who can't be proud of their true personality.

Mr. Been with Everybody and Back _(refer back to Mr. Player)_

To start with… we know that this guy type sounds a tad ratchet but in our defense you need to be warned (lol ☺)! Mr. Been with everybody and back may have a resemblance to Mr. Player… without Mr. Player's smoothness of course. This mister basically describes those guys that may have dated you, your cousin, your sister, your best friend, your not so best friend, your cousin's best friend, and that girl in your first period that sits on the front row and gives you funny looks. Mr. Been with everybody and back isn't necessarily charming but may have some characteristics that catch your eye. Like Mr. Player they do not care for your benefit specifically, but they care about what they can get from you. These types normally already have a bad reputation, so if you hear something about him maybe you should take it to heart instead of thinking everyone's a hater (remember a lady must pick and choose her battles refer to rule #60).

To be real these misters are just nasty and a young lady doesn't deserve that. You deserve a guy that cares for you and not you, your cousin, the girl down the block, and secretly wants your best friend. Trust me we know that's why we're talking about it. Don't deny the rumors, because in his case they are probably true.

Mr. Almost Perfect SIKE NAW Not Really

Again with the long names but this one is a must and a necessary to explain, me and my sister must do our job to warn you of the shamefulness of this mister! With that being said, "Mr. Almost Perfect SIKE NAW Not Really" is a bootleg "Prince Charming". He is just what we described..."almost perfect but not really". For instance, say you meet this guy who is potentially perfect and he has all the qualities you are looking for and it seems like nothing can go wrong, but to your tragic dismay you find out he already has a girlfriend even though he was treating you like his so called girlfriend. You may feel disappointed and upset with yourself because you allowed this trickery to happen, but don't because almost perfect is reaaaallyy close to perfect (especially since Mr. Perfect doesn't exist).

This is a basic act of deception and it happens to the best and worst of us. Just remember "almost doesn't count"... not when it comes to matters of the heart anyway. Beware of this mister and watch for signs of his clever trickery such as inconvenient lies, avoidance, and sudden changes. Mr. Almost Perfect SIKE NAW Not Really is liable to blinding a girl's eyes with his fake interpretation of love, so as a lady know what you want and don't settle for less or what "seems" like more. If you come across this mister don't let him change your perception of males because all males aren't bad and they aren't all "almost perfect". So really take caution or you will be telling yourself SIKE NAW!

Mr. Best Friend

Every girl deserves a guy best friend and sometime some feelings may develop between you two. At first it may be scary very scary but don't panic it's pretty normal. It's normally because he gives special attention and he holds you down and always lends a listening ear. He may be sweet, understanding and most the time your parents will like him. He thinks you're pretty when you don't think so and you are both of the opposite sex so sometimes flirting might happen between yall. But mixing love and friendship can be dangerous very dangerous. Try to remember to follow your heart and make the right decision pertaining to this situation. Also be aware that some guys only get close to you so they can make their move. I know this is deceitful and sneaky but some guys would go that far to get a girl. If you do develop strong feelings for your best friend and you decide to make a move try to be understanding if the guy choose not to want to take it far. Respect that decision and remember that you too started as just friends in the first place.

Mr. Now or Later

This is one of our favorite types of guys ever :). Mr. 'Now or Later is hard on the outside (the now) and soft on the inside (the later)? Mr. Now or Later is a guy that seems hard and tough on the outside but when you get to know him he is truly soft with a heart of gold. You may think...why would this type of guy be a good thing? Well first off you have to try to understand why he acts hard in the first place. It may be hard to believe that guys can be romantically hurt but some are, and some may carry unresolved issues at home, or other baggage (just like us girls).

So if you ever encounter one, then remember to try to be patient with him because the benefits of waiting will be great :). We firmly believe in the quotes "_anything worth having is worth fighting for_" and "_good things come to those who wait_", so keep those in mind also. We also compiled a list of things that will help you determine whether you are dealing with this type of guy: He may be distant, maybe seem unemotional, may fear commitment, and maybe even try to act like Mr. Player (refer to Mister #2) in order to mask the hurt he may be feeling. Just remember that patience is everything when dealing with this type, but don't wait forever either. A heart of gold is terrible to waste but tearing through concrete to find it is not always the best decision.

Mr. Social Site

Mr. Social site... Oh how we shake our head at them (smh). They are the type of guys that we laugh at when we read their status. They are the type who probably will get their quotes off search engines (at least they sound like it) and they always have a bunch of Social site likes too (20-30+). These are the guys that use Social sites to get girls and gain popularity. Normally their statuses say something sweet and romantic...they would make you say aw, or some status would make you think they are deep when in reality they are not. *EX.) "The best curve on a girl's body is her smile."* These types of guys based their "fame" off of Social sites. AVOID RELATIONSHIP WITH THESE GUYS!!! Reason being is because they will put the whole relationship on Social sites and that is not a good thing, your business is your business and remember to keep it as such (refer to rule #25 statuses).

Mr. Ain't About That Life

I know this title may seem a tad ghetto and a bit illiterate but I think it fits the situation. This is a bad type of guy and you should never ever get into a relationship with this type. So here's the true explanation of Mr.Ain'tAboutThatLife. He is the type of guy that starts to act funny after you two start to get close. More than likely as soon as you hit the 5 month mark in the relationship or as soon as you too start to embrace unknown emotions he starts to freeze up on you. We have even heard from friends that this sometimes happens after you make out with him or partake in sexual activities.

Basically, this Mister fails to mean what he says and say what he means, hence him not being about that life (that loyal relationship life, that commitment life, etc.). This could even be described as the guy who fails to take care of his responsibilities (often times this is the Mister single moms had met up with... and YOU DON'T WANT THAT). In some instances he can often resemble Mr. Almost Perfect Sike Naw Not Really or Mr. Deceiver.

In the event that you do encounter this type of

guy and you fall for his charm, smooth talking, lies and cleverness try not to beat yourself up about it. This happens to the best of us. Remember that God has a good guy in store for you and sometimes you have to experience the bad to appreciate the good. So try and make sure your potential boyfriend is about that life... whatever productive life you would want him to live up too lol.

Mr. I'm Sweet but over Flirty

Alright this one is pretty self-explanatory but we felt this type needs be briefly discussed. This type of guy may fall into the category of Mr. Player and definitely Mr. Almost Perfect SIKE NAW Not Really. He seems sooo sweet, charming and smooth and he seems perfect right? He seems like he has everything together? But the one problem is he FLIRT too much and he flirts with too many people and sometimes he may even come at you in an overly sexual way. This type is **NO GOOD!!!** This type is also very confusing to understand because you can never tell their true intentions so just stay away from this type...trust us on this one.

Mr. Compare You to His Ex's

We are all girls so we all know that we greatly DISLIKE to be compared to someone no matter who they are (you know since we're special and all☺). Hence, it is a terrible feeling to be compared to your boyfriend's or crushes previous girlfriend. It feels like a slap on the face when he mentions his previous girlfriends anyway and it definitely feels bad when he says you remind him of her. The best way to handle this type of guy is to talk to him. Sit down and have a serious heart-to-heart and explain to him clearly what he did and how it makes you feel (because most guys don't read between the lines... unfortunately). Also, talk to each other in a calm voice and in a mature manner. Make sure you open up and lay it all on the table; this will also help with the two of you communication skills. Work it out and work through it and be patient with the results because as the old saying goes "Rome wasn't built in a day".

Mr. Talk It and Walk It

Does this mister sound familiar? If so, it's probably because he sounds like the common and oh so talked about "Mr. Hit it and Quit it". But, unlike "Mr. Hit and Quit it", Mr. Talk It and Walk It doesn't refer to sex. This Mister is that common crush you get, and as soon as you really start to like him, or get feelings for him, or even start responding to his received sincerity ... they just disappear. It's sort of like they are stealing companionship, feelings, kisses, and all that other mushy stuff us girls like in guys. He can talk that talk, meaning he may seem like he knows all your favorite things, knows how to make you smile, and even understands your feelings (let's be real guys will never understand the feelings of a female... we're different for a reason you know☺). To our puzzlement, after he wastes all that effort to "talk" ... He "walks".

This is when the conversations stop, the sweet sayings lessen, and ultimate contact is ceased until you two become strangers. WARNING: DO NOT FALL BACK INTO CRUSH MODE WITH THIS MISTER AFTER HE WALKS IT! (He is liable to come back as Mr. Hit it and Quit it, and let's not even get started with the rachetness of this mister... trust me you don't want that memory in your life). Mr. Talk it and Walk It is normally ran into more nowadays due to you know Social site relationships, and internet friendships (because friendship over the web is never guaranteed anyway).

Our advice is to not keep your guard up and shut people from your life because you're afraid they will walk (... trust me self-pity never works) but to be cautious of who your feelings go out to and of course not to start tripping over someone all of a sudden (you know being sprung). Emotions are like invitations to your heart, and if a guy wants to open the invitation without coming to the party (that is your heart)... or too say this in a less poetic way: If a guy backs up after getting close to you in any way then he obviously wasn't right for you so when he leaves don't beat yourself up about it, just know…you didn't need them anyway lol. Take this Mister as a lesson learned for yourself, for other girls who may experience this, and even future relationships. But DO NOT let it make you bitter towards males, just let it make you stronger in life itself. In other words make sure your mister is **bout that life!** Also refer to Mr. Ain't about That Life.

Mr. Rebound

For all you basketball fans we know that a rebound is when you gain possession over the ball off the backboard or rim after an unsuccessful shot (You like that basketball knowledge). In life a rebound is a spring back after an unsuccessful event (funny how sports can teach us things... Who would have thought? lol). And that brings me to the definition of Mr. Rebound, a guy who uses yall "love", feelings, whatever you two got going on... and you all's relationship as a way to get over his ex, this is also referee to as *frontin'*. This ladies is not good at all, especially considering that many may even use you to make their exes jealous. AVOID THESE TYPES!! They will not do anything but break your heart & create unnecessary drama in your life.

But let's not forget that girls do it too. You know how the phrase goes... **"The best way to get over a guy is to get a new guy"** (says the trifling best friend character in most movies after her best friend gets dumped by the one who held her heart smh -_ -). This phrase must stop! It is not cute when a male does this to us females; likewise, it is not cute when a female does the same thing (smh).

So just try to avoid being a rebound girl, if a guy wants to put up a front then you are not obligated to be his cover-up. A real man handles his baggage and emotions just like a real lady picks and choose her battles (refer to rule #60 & Mr. Been with Everybody and Back). The best way to duck out this mister would be to avoid being with a guy who just broke up with his girl (that is just drama waiting to explode!). If he is serious he will wait ... until his attention aren't on a PAST and present relationship. Time tells all and remember the past is to learn from not to revisit!!

Mr. Emotional

Aaaaaaahhh... here it goes with this one. We as young ladies dread this Mister, love this Mister, and yet relate so well to this Mister because us ladies knows how it feels to be emotional and sometimes we take things over board which causes us to be over emotional & over dramatic. But it's even harder to think that guys may act the same way (refer to Mr. Now and Later) and this we call Mr. Emotional. Now... don't get us wrong a guy that is emotional isn't all that bad. You don't want him to be a meanie, but you don't want him to act like you either, right? We know, it's confusing but also be aware that sometimes their emotional outbreaks might start to annoy you.

Most girls say they want a guy that's sensitive but remember that as a young lady going through hormonal changes, indecisiveness, and ultimately trying to find out whom in the world we are that your emotions may be too much to handle without even adding on the extra tote bag that is his emotions too! You may not even know what you want so just find someone that balances you out.

For example, if you're a laid-back girl then maybe you need Mr. Emotional to keep you in perspective and attached. On the other hand, if you're already a rainbow of emotions waiting to explode then Mr. Emotional will not be a good choice, in this case you probably want a Mr. Nice and Easy so someone can help manage that roller coaster of emotions you got going on ;). The decision is up to you, but pick wisely... and when dealing with Mr. Emotional remember to listen, understand, be kind, and let him know when enough is enough! (Since he is emotional... he may or may not understand, we don't predict the future so we don't know lol)

Mr. Meanie

Okay so this mister may sound a bit childish because we know we used the word meanie in like 1st grade lol, but in describing this mister we want to be polite so here is Mr. Meanie. This is pretty self-explanatory; Mr. Meanie is well.... mean lol. He is the guy that walks around with a chip on his shoulder, the one who thinks everyone is judging him, the one who thinks everyone owes him something just because he has a negative attitude. Actually, Mr. Meanie strongly resembles Miss. Bitter... you know how we are when we get attitudes, we don't wanna talk, we don't wanna listen, and we don't wanna care in fact we just don't wanna lol.

Mr. Meanie is the same way, except his attitude is more so in guy form (I know scary huh?). Beware of this type; he is usually laid-back on the outside and uncaring on the inside. Mr. Meanie often makes you feel sorry for his saga or whatever soap opera he has going on in his life at the time. In remembering to take into account others feelings know that you cannot carry others issues on your back.... that is God's job not yours. Don't feel like you have to stick with Mr. Meanie because "you're the only one that understands him" or because "he don't treat you like he does others". Everyone has a sensitive side but it's not necessary to have to dig through the concrete to find out (refer to Mr. Thug). Mr. Meanie needs to work on his self so he will know how to treat a lady because **THEY DON'T KNOW HOW TO DO SO!** While he goes to therapy to get his act together you continue to be kind and compassionate yet practical and sensible. Don't get us wrong, Mr. Meanie can be sweet and when he is it feels like your heart is glowing. But it's all temporary; he may also be cold, distant, and troubled. The point is Mr. Meanie is not for you Miss Lady.

Oh and that saying "For every man is a woman that will make him change"... we don't know how liable that is so please don't use this to support your Mr. Meanie. We know that only God can change a person's heart and in order for anyone to change they must want it first. Yes you can influence Mr. Meanie but you cannot transform him into Mr. Good Guy (we will speak on him later :)). Take your kindness elsewhere or you will be a sick puppy, feeling lonely, unappreciated, and even having low self-esteem. On a serious note it's not worth it and no one deserves this. **WARNING: THIS**

MISTER MAY RESULT IN ABUSE (physical, mental, verbal, etc...) AVOID THIS AT ALL COSTS! You don't have to stay with anyone, especially not a Mr. Meanie!

Mr. Controlling *(refer back to Mr. Meanie)*

This Mister is often just like Mr. Meanie, but on a serious note we want to warn you all by saying ignore, avoid, and stay away from this mister. You may be attracted to his assertiveness and ability to make you feel like he has everything under control (much like Mr. Thug), but this will all go downhill in the end because he really wants to destroy you and your inner beauty. Mr. Controlling does not want to see you succeed unless of course it has something to do with him (if it doesn't have anything to do with him then he will make it seem as such). In other words, Mr. Controlling will destroy you because he doesn't really care for you. Mr. controlling is normally seen as Mr. Abuser, because they want to take over every aspect of your life. So don't think it's cute when he is ALWAYS asking where you are and who you are with? It's not because he cares it's because he wants that control. Also, don't think because you're young an abusive relationship is nonexistent it happens to young ladies all the time. Don't let that be, you leave at the first signs of this; it will pay off in the long run.

Mr. One Word

To start with this one let's discuss how there are so many forms of technology and so many diverse ways to communicate. We can talk, chat, email, video, call, etc... Typically, nowadays we can just send a quick little text message and call it a day. And as girls we send the long, elaborate texts expressing feelings or even just asking him how his day went... and he has the audacity to send you back one word, For example, "OMG! I missed you, you miss me?" **"Yea"** "How was your day! Tell me all about it :)" **"It was straight"** "Oh okay well love you" **"Ily 2"**

What a shame right!? That is very annoying and it makes it hard to keep up the conversation.... this is none other than Mr. One Word himself! All he basically says is **k, lol, aight, good, cool, nothing, wbu (**what about you**)**, oh and the occasional and much better (we meant that sarcastically of course) **that's what's up.** SMH he is an illiterate tragedy and a shame to texters everywhere. He is worse than Mr. Ain't About that Life, he is just Mr. One Word (smh it even sounds boring when you type it...). So here is our advice on this type of guy: Don't try to get in a relationship with him because more than likely it will fail due to the lack of communication (can't really communicate with one word can you?) Communication is vital to any relationship and that is what this mister lacks.... communication, talking, basic people skills! If you happen to have a crush on this Mister don't fret, all that will go down the drain after about two months of dry conversation. If you're impatient like me, more like 3 weeks lol. Also, don't force this boring person to talk because one worders will always be one worders, we're pretty sure you've experienced this with the average texter, so we know you want to avoid that in a relationship.

Mr. Wannabe Rapper aka Mr. Dreamer

We all have aspirations and dreams that we hope to fulfill and achieve. Most women say they want a guy who has dreams and aspirations too because that means they want something out of life. As females we all want to be the one who helps motivate him to achieve his goals in life. A guy who is a dreamer is a great thing but lately when a guy is a dreamer he wants to be a rapper or a pro-ball player and don't get us wrong there is nothing wrong with that at all and if that's his dream support it and be there for him. But if you are really serious about him make sure he has a backup plan so he want spend his whole life chase a faraway dream. And again we aren't saying that he can't be the next famous star. We are just saying that remember that everybody can't be this and that if he doesn't succeed in fulfilling his dreams remember to be there through it all.

Mr. All (his) Friends Are Girls

This is a guy that most females encounter in their life and some of you who are reading this book might have already experienced this. So I'm going to go ahead and break this down. So you have a guy friend that you really like but it seems as if there are always some girls in his face and he claims they're just friends and they may just be that to him, just FRIENDS!! Try not to be jealous and we know it's hard because as females we don't like the thought of sharing or the thought that he may like some other girl more than you but you have to respect his friendships. Whenever you feel insecure about where you stand with him because of all his girl-friends try to remember that you're his girl and he likes you and keep that in mind. Try to avoid fights and arguments over this situation but don't be afraid to open up and tell how you in a CALM way ladies (no yelling please) feel. But the most important thing to remember about this type that some people don't know or don't consider that every guy that is like this is a cheater that is not true. Don't get us wrong some are but not all, so just follow your heart and pray for the best and if he does cheat it wasn't meant to be and God has something better in mind for you.

WARNING: If a guy has majority of girls as just friends but, he calls most of them his "sisters" and they spend too much time together and he tells them more than he tells you and she is ALWAYS in his face (texting him, tweeting him, tagging him in pictures, posting on his social site wall every five minutes talking about some "Sister & Bro for life to the end no matter what") then it's usually more than her being like his sister. Remember family normally isn't that close so fake family surely wouldn't be!

Mr. Love Don't Cost a Thing

Okay so, I know this is a weird title and you probably don't know what this means. Here is a little background info: ☺ there once was a stereotypical nerd (a real nerd doesn't have to be, look, or act like that) who became popular and cool by a pretty and popular girl at his school. Long story short, once he got popular he started acting brand new (he changed for the worst) and forgot who made him that way... they fell in love in the end (kissy kissy goo goo), but in real life it may not go like that so here is our warning. Mr. Love Don't Cost A Thing is the mister who wasn't all of that or all of nothing until you came along. You know the type... he didn't have a circle of friends who hung out after school until he got his trophy girlfriend. If you are in this situation then please LEAVE the situation. It is not worth your time if your partner is ungrateful, selfish, or fake.

If you took out the time to be with someone and it ended up benefiting them then they owe you their respect because you didn't have to do that. We don't mean to sound shallow or harsh but in real life people will forget where they came from. In the long run these people usually fall apart (just like in the movie...TRUUUEEEEE!) and these are the people that may have lost sight of what is important and as growing young ladies YOU DON'T HAVE TIME to wait for people to realize their values. So get it together and move on and usually they will come to their senses just don't wait for it or expect it because life doesn't always work like you expect. On the bright side it's always nice to see good things come from the nice things you do for people, so even though they may not always show their gratitude always treat people right.

Mr. No Commitment

Here we go with this one... I'm sure you all know this mister or have seen him in the common romantic comedy film. Mr. No commitment is one who just will not get into a relationship, or he will never take you seriously. You all could be blindly in love or even soul-mates (theoretically) but he will never ever ever truly see that or he will just ignore this. We all have experienced this in one way or another. You know the guy who you do all those favors for, and spend all that time on the phone with and he is still clueless to the fact that you all would be perfect in a relationship! Our advice to you is... don't bet on this happening, life is not a fairy tale. Mr. No commitment will do just that, HE WILL NOT COMMIT! Some will eventually, but it will take a long time (a long time as in 7-15 years!).

These are the couples that you may know personally as well. You know that aunt that's been with her boyfriend for about nine years, and the whole family knows him, and you even call him uncle... but in reality your aunt is not even married to this individual. She has a no committer and she will end up with no commitment. In our opinion, we suggest that you don't wait past that three year mark, and if you've known each other since grade school then the circumstances are different. But, it doesn't take forever to know a person and it doesn't take a lifetime to be in a relationship. So do not waste your time because I'm sure there is another Mister out there who isn't a procrastinator or no committer. Remember we young ladies are precious and so it takes Mr. Good guy to realize that, not Mr. No Commitment.

Mr. Good Guy aka The Realistic Prince Charming

Mr. Good Guy is the Mister we should all be aiming for, but because we can get a little superficial we often want Mr. Gorgeous with a nice body or Mr. Prince Charming or Mr. Baller/Shot Caller. Let us tell you about Mr. Good Guy (YAAAAAAAAAAAAAYY!!!). Mr. Good Guy is probably not what you think he is. Because to our disbelief he isn't going to be ultra popular (these are the bad types anyway) or super attractive but they are surely going to have a good heart and a good mind with goals, ambitions, and they are going to actually succeed (and not sit around like Mr. Wannabe Rapper or Mr. Dreamer). THIS IS WHAT MATTERS PEOPLE! It's not going to be easy having Mr. Good Guy because you all might have arguments or you may feel like he cares way too much (refer back to Mr. Emotional), but no relationship is perfect and you must KNOW that. We ourselves can't even fully explain Mr. Good Guy because we haven't encountered him that much (because we get superficial too).

If we have encountered them then we obviously don't know it, often times Mr. Good

Guy is right there in front of us just like the movies say. All we are saying is Mr. Good Guy is your soul-mate, he is the one that is heaven sent and is the one actually worth fighting for and because he is Mr. Good Guy the fight won't be a total headache. If you are a youngn' reading this book then Mr. Good Guy may look like the one who shares his animal crackers with you when you don't have any left (AAAAAWWW).

In brief, be on the lookout for Mr. Good Guy and as our mothers say pray for Mr. Good Guy now. He is the realistic prince charming, he will have a career and appreciate you along with the flaws that we all have. Mr. Good Guy will always have a sense of humor (you can't be with someone you think is boring) and keep you motivated as you should him. So, for a little history lesson, you all may remember some of the shows with the perfect family, the husband was everything you want in a man… yea he was Mr. Good Guy hence his perfect life that we all want lol. In hindsight, Mr. Good Guy is your future husbands so please don't miss out and we will try not to do the same (we are learning to :))

Real Recognize Real
The real experts give advice for young girls on life:

Janice Pigford

My advice to pre teens and teenagers would be to endure their school work with patience and perseverance, and to work hard at their education. Education is the most important avenue to success and the future. **Keep your self-esteem and confidence at a high level** and know that you are important and you will achieve your goals.

Susan Bizzell

My advice to young females is when all else fails just let go and let God. Pray for wisdom, knowledge and understanding and try to keep in mind that all things work together for the good of those who love the Lord (Romans 8:28). Remember to keep God first in your life and all the rest of your priorities will fall into place. Continue to walk in the favor of God and continue to uphold the standards of a virtuous, Christian young woman (Proverbs 31) and keep the faith no matter what life throws at you.

You're still young and remember that everything you do today can affect your future so choose wisely and be careful of what you say. The things you say and do today might come back to you in the future so many politicians and celebrities' text and take picture that end up being publicize don't let that be you. Don't text or take any picture that you wouldn't want anybody to see because one day everybody might know. Carry yourself as a lady at all times.

Petula Jones

Girls and Young Ladies, this is the most precious time of your life. Girls, you are to obey your parents and respect them. God said, Children obey your parents in the Lord, for this is right. Ephesians 6:1 Girls, never allow anyone to have you to do something that your parents told you that was wrong and never pick on or talk about anyone because you can cause that individual to have low self-esteem about themselves. Girls always act like little girls, and not older than what you are. Enjoy your time as girls, and set goals for yourself at this age. Always have a positive attitude, that you are who God created you to be and that is **"Precious In His Sight"**.

To the Young Ladies, always, always carry yourself as young ladies who is unique and beautiful, never think of yourself as "less than" but you are "more than" meets the eye. Be that young lady who stand outs and not the one that fits in. Because when you stand out from the rest you are different from the rest. Have a mind of a winner and not a loser, a winner is someone who is positive, set goals and plan for the future. A loser is someone who thinks negative, no goals and no plans for their future. I can say when I was 17, I was a loser because I did things that a loser would do. I hung around losers, that didn't listen to their parents and talked back to their parents. And I did the same thing, and would sneak out of the house to be with a boy. I ended up pregnant at the age of 17 … But I kept that from my mom and end up losing the baby. Young ladies don't get involve while you are in high school because it will cause you to lose focus on everything you wanted to do, be that winner God created you to be. Life is good!!...

Heart to Heart
A little advice and encouragement from girls just like you:

Cashmir Fountain

Nowadays girls let everything get to their head. It's okay to have a little fun in life, but make sure you have a destination in life. I thought I could have fun first and put school later but that doesn't work. In order to get anywhere in life you need to try, at least give yourself that much. Don't rush through life either, you have your whole life ahead of you, and also act your age. If you're a preteen don't try to be an adult that early just live your life.

Latrice Thompson

As a young child, I quickly realized that college wasn't something that was guaranteed to me. Raised solely by my grandmother, she had plenty of problems that didn't even concern my education. Scraping by just to put food on the table, college just didn't seem that important. Not that she didn't care; she was just literally exhausted working day and night just to take care of an entire family and a young girl with a fiery attitude (me). Although college wasn't usually encouraged in my home, I was determined to make it one way or another. This made me come to the realization that I was different.

I had goals and dreams, something that a lot of people in my family had simply let go. Instead of following the path of my family members who struggled each and every day, I dared to be different. I made up my mind that I was going to do whatever it took to make something of myself and that's exactly what I did. Years later, I am on my way to Florida Atlantic University to major in Nursing. Not only am I doing that, I hope to soon own my own clinic or hospital. The sky is the limit and as I soar I plan to take my grandmother along with me. Just because my past wasn't promising doesn't mean my future can't be. I didn't let my surroundings nor do my situations affect my goals. You can do ANYTHING you set your mind to. A little faith and determination will take you a long way. I am a walking example.

W.A.I.T.
(We Are Inactive Teens)

Our Mission

Our mission is to educate, inform and inspire teens to postpone sexual activity and focus on more positive things that will equip them for a successful future. Our goal is to equip our teens with the necessary information and inspiration that will enable them to focus on their dreams, their goals and their purpose for life. We are also an information center that will help keep youths abreast of a variety of positive opportunities that will help enhance their life as we network with other groups, clubs and organization that focus on bringing out the best in our teens.

About Us

WAIT is an organization founded by Ministers Dexter and Petula Jones and the President is Jasmine S. Jones, the organization focus on celibacy as the only 100 percent effective way to preventing pregnancy and contracting STD. WAIT stands for We Are Inactive Teens. Our goal is to educate and show teens through educational and motivational programs geared toward promoting knowledge and inspiration to wait. We do this by reinforcing self-confidence and positive values, goals, dreams, purpose and attitudes as an important prerequisite. We are available to conduct seminars and workshops at schools, churches, after-school programs, teen-retreats, etc... We also teach about relationship building, STD, pregnancy, and abstinence. The time has come to take back our teens through education, inspiration, and eventually celebration as we see our teens that are sexually active go from being sexually active to celibacy with the idea to abstain from all sexual activity until marriage. And those that are virgins remaining so until their wedding day and keeping themselves holy for the glory of God and their future life partner and soul mate in marriage.

"CELIBACY IS THE ONLY 100% EFFECTIVE WAY TO PREVENT OUT-OF-WEDLOCK PREGNANCY AND STD."

CHECK OUT OUR WEBSITE AND EMAIL AT:
www.waituntilmarried.org / teens.wait@gmail.com

www.ingramcontent.com/pod-product-compliance
Lightning Source LLC
Chambersburg PA
CBHW061448040426
42450CB00007B/1273